Never
Sleep
With The
Director
And 50 other
Ridiculous Film Rules

5/9/2014

Dearest Esther,

just make your own
rules as director for
your documentaries and
your life.

You did a great job!

Much love, dad.

COLOPHON

BIS Publishers
Het Sieraad
Postjesweg 1
1057 DT Amsterdam
The Netherlands
T (+) 31 (0)20-515 02 30
F (+) 31 (0)20-515 02 39
bis@bispublishers.nl
www.bispublishers.nl

ISBN 978-90-6369-276-6

Ridiculous Design Rules is a concept developed
by Lemon Scented Tea and commissioned by
Premsela, Dutch Platform for Design and Fashion
(www.premsela.org).

Editorial Director: Anneloes van Gaalen
(www.paperdollwriting.com)
Designed by: Lilian van Dongen Torman
(www.lilianvandongentorman.nl)
Proofreading: Sarina Ruiter-Bouwhuis

BIS PUBLISHERS

Never Sleep With The Director

And 50 other
Ridiculous Film Rules

CONTENTS

INTRODUCTION

From its inception in the late nineteenth century, the movies have captured our collective imagination. Over the years the technology has changed, as have the 'rules' that filmmakers adhere to. High time to shine some light on film-related tips, tricks and mishaps.

This book is meant for movie lovers, silver-screen starlets and the people who get to yell 'cut' and 'action' on set. It contains 51 movie-related rules, their history and quotes by industry leaders, Hollywood big shots, indie directors and a whole list of actors and actresses.

The rules range from helpful tips for editors – "Kill your darlings" – to words of wisdom aimed at directors – "Never work with animals or children." From horror movie clichés – "Never pick up the phone" – to the ridiculous rules of the old Hollywood Production Code – "No picture shall be produced which will lower the moral standards of those who see it" – right down to sound advice for any struggling actor or actress – "Never sleep with the director."

Ridiculous Film Rules is the sixth book in a series that focuses on rules that people working in the creative industry – graphic designers, fashion designers, advertisers, typographers and filmmakers – can rely on, or ignore altogether. Future publications include *Ridiculous Photography Rules* and *Ridiculous Art Rules*.

Also visit www.ridiculousrules.com.

never sleep with the director

It might be tempting for a struggling actor or actress to sleep his or her way to the top. Likewise, a director could easily fall for his or her leading lady or man. But as attractive as it might seem to share your bed, or trailer, with the object of your on-set affection, it generally serves the movie and your career best to keep some professional distance.

"The ladder of success in Hollywood is usually a press agent, actor, director, producer, leading man; and you are a star if you sleep with each of them in that order. Crude, but true."
Hedy Lamarr (1914-2000), Austrian-American actress

"Never fuck the talent."
Charlton Heston (1923-2008), American actor

"It's a little daunting when you're doing a love scene with somebody else and your husband says something like, 'That was terrific darling, but I know you can do it better.'"
Julie Andrews (1935), British actress

"Never fall in love with your leading lady!"
Wim Wenders (1945), German director

"Having sex with any member of your cast is a bad idea – crew is better."
John Waters (1946), American director

"If someone's playing my character, I have to be in love with her to some degree. It's not so much about lust, but I have to adore her."
Quentin Tarantino (1963), American director

"It looks like a clever ruse getting together with a film director. Unfortunately, it's not that simple. Tim [Burton] is unbelievably disciplined about employing me only if I am absolutely right. For Sweeney Todd, it was like I had to be more right than anyone else; it was 'in spite of', instead of 'because of', being his girlfriend."
Helena Bonham Carter (1966), British actress

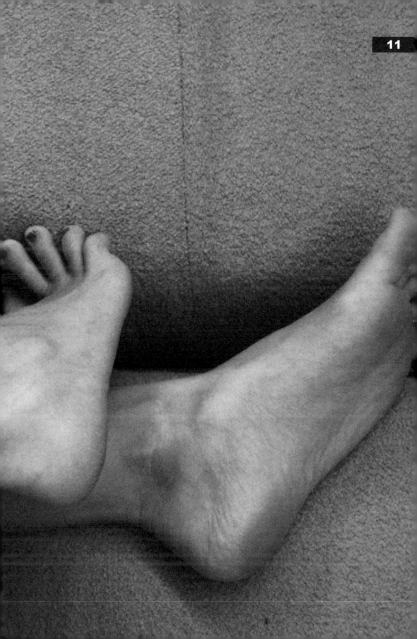

The book will always be better

In 2010 posters with Oscar reading a book started popping up both online and in the city of Amsterdam. The posters, which read 'the book was better,' were made by Dutch designer Woes van Haaften (of Incl.) who wanted to visually communicate the close relationship that exists between the world of books and film: "March traditionally is the month of the Oscars and the annual Dutch Book Ball. The two worlds are connected in one respect because both books and films are cultural products that tell a story. On the other hand, these worlds compete with each other. When a book is adapted for the screen, it's only a matter of time before reviews come out stating that 'the book was better' than the film. By unifying both events we had the ultimate ground to motivate the public to consider this cliché."

"A movie is not a book. If the source material is a book, you cannot be too respectful of the book. All you owe to the book is the spirit."
Graham Greene (1904-1991), British author

"When I do a novel, I don't really use the script, I use the book; when I did *Apocalypse Now*, I used *Heart of Darkness*. Novels usually have so much rich material."
Francis Ford Coppola (1939), American director

"Don't adapt novels."
Wim Wenders (1945), German director

"I never see a novel as a film while I'm writing it. Mostly because novels and films are so different, and I'm such an internal novelist."
Alice Hoffman (1952), American author

THE BOOK WAS BETTER

SHOW, DON'T TELL

This rule actually comes from the world of writing. The idea is that you don't just tell your reader what is going on, but paint a picture using words so that they can really feel part of the story. Because film is a visual medium, you'd think that showing rather than telling would come natural. Unfortunately, there are still plenty of directors who insist on jam packing their cinematic endeavor with static conversational scenes that are heavy in dialogue and short on action.

"When we tell a story in cinema, we should resort to dialogue only when it's impossible to do otherwise. I always try first to tell a story in the cinematic way, through a succession of shots and bits of film in between… Dialogue should simply be a sound among sounds, just something that comes out of the mouths of people whose eyes tell the story in visual terms."
Alfred Hitchcock (1899-1980),
British director

"I think people remember pictures, not dialogue. That's why I like pictures."
David Lean (1908-1991), British director

"The aesthetics of film are 80 percent visual, 20 percent auditory... The best advice for writing film dialogue is don't. Never write a line of dialogue when you can create a visual expression."
Robert McKee (1941), American screenwriting lecturer

"The right image or look can replace a page of dialogue."
Steven Zaillian (1953), Armenian-American screenwriter and director

"I'm kind of pissed off about all these PG-13 movies that aren't scary, that are not efficient. They don't show you anything. 'Less is more' is the bullshit everyone at the studios is feeding you. No! I want to see it! If I don't see anything, I can't get into the movie."
Alexandre Aja (1978), French film director

Kill your darlings

It's a well-known movie mantra that has its origins in the world of writing. Credits usually go to American writer William Faulkner (1897-1962), who once said: "In writing, you must kill your darlings." But it was British writer Sir Arthur Quiller-Couch (1863-1944) who first coined the term "murder your darlings" back in 1916. Sir Arthur, who at the time served as Professor of English at Cambridge University, argued in a series of lectures titled *On the Art of Writing* that "whenever you feel an impulse to perpetrate a piece of exceptionally fine writing, obey it – whole-heartedly – and delete it before sending your manuscripts to press. Murder your darlings."

"Kill your darlings, kill your darlings, even when it breaks your egocentric little scribbler's heart. Kill your darlings."
Stephen King (1947), American author

"Save your darlings, kill the editor."
Campaign by Screenvision

"You kill the thing that you're really attached to, which is hard. It's part of the process, because in the end you hope it'll make what you have stronger."
Josh Cooley (1979), story artist at Pixar Animation Studios

Have fun

Have fun. On paper it's the simplest rule to remember, but according to American director Eli Roth (1972) it's also the easiest to forget: "You have to have fun or what's the point? And sometimes you need to be reminded of that. So go out for crew drinks. Laugh and share playback on the monitor with everyone when you've filmed a great kill. And do that extra take for fun, even though you know you've got the shot, just for the love of making movies."

———

"We're supposed to have so much fun, like puppy dogs with our tails wagging. It's supposed to be a great living; it's supposed to be fantastic."
David Lynch (1946), American director

"You can't take yourself too seriously. I think it's something you see all the time. As a result, a lot of really talented directors are gone now. I pray every day that I never get to that point."
John Carpenter (1948), American director

"I had more fun making *Traffic* than either of the Ocean's films."
Steven Soderbergh (1963), American producer and director

Less is more

Architect Ludwig Mies van der Rohe (1886-1969) is generally considered to have coined the phrase 'less is more.' But in all fairness, the motto was first mentioned back in 1855 in a poem by Robert Browning (1812-1889) titled *Andrea del Sarto*. In the world of film, the 'less is more' principle not only means deleting scenes in order to make an epic-length film more suitable for an attention-deficit audience. It also means reducing visual trickery, attention-grabbing décor or overly explanatory narratives in an effort to leave something up to the audience's imagination.

"The length of a film should be directly related to the endurance of the human bladder."
Alfred Hitchcock (1899-1980), British director

"No comedy should be longer than 90 minutes. There's no such thing as a good long joke."
John Waters (1946), American director

"Suspense is like a woman. The more left to the imagination, the more the excitement."

Alfred Hitchcock (1899-1980), British director

"One thing I learned in the editing room is that less is usually more."
Steven Zaillian (1953), Armenian-American screenwriter and director

"I'm always very suspicious of things that give away too much, I'm very much a 'less is more' school of narrative and information."
Ed Gass-Donnelly (1977), Canadian director

"I'm not a huge proponent of 'less is more'; I think when you do a movie, you have to create an immersion for the audience. You have to make a movie where the audience [members] feel like they are living the story and not only watching something."
Alexandre Aja (1978), French film director

Dress the part

There are few enviable careers in which grown men and women get paid money to play dress-up and pretend to be somebody they're not. To reduce the noble art of acting to a dress-up game for grown-ups would be ridiculous. But the fact remains that in order to act the part, you need to dress the part.

"It was because of Garbo that I left MGM. In her last picture they wanted to make her a sweater girl, a real American type. I said, 'When the glamour ends for Garbo, it also ends for me. She has created a type. If you destroy that illusion, you destroy her.' When Garbo walked out of the studio, glamour went with her, and so did I."
Adrian (1903-1959), American costume designer

"Acting is just a matter of farting about in disguises."
Peter O'Toole (1932), Irish actor

"I've been a zombie, a vampire, and a squid. It's quite nice to play someone in a normal pair of trousers."
Bill Nighy (1949), British actor

"Character development is at the forefront of costume design. The characters move the story along and, with the director and the actor, the costume designer helps to set the film's emotional tone in a visual way."
Jeffrey Kurland (1952), American costume designer

"I got to dress up in funny clothes and run around New Zealand with a bow and arrow for 18 months, how bad could that be?"
Orlando Bloom (1977), British actor

Forget -the- Film, Watch -the- Titles

rule
08

It's both a rule and the name of a website that is filled to the brim with title sequences. The site, which was launched by Amsterdam-based production company Submarine in 2006, celebrates the art of film title design in an effort to show that "the very best title sequences... are the signifiers of contemporary pop culture and an art form in their own right." We couldn't agree more.

"My initial thoughts about what a title can do was to set the mood and the prime underlying core of the film's story, to express the story in some metaphorical way. I saw the title as a way of conditioning the audience, so that when the film actually began, viewers would already have an emotional resonance with it".
Saul Bass (1920-1996), American graphic designer

"I believe that a great title sequence almost literally hypnotizes you."
Ken Coupland (1947-2005), Canadian writer

"I call [the credit sequence] 'crack for designers.' It's got everything: the glamour of Hollywood, motion and color and sound."
Ken Coupland (1947-2005), Canadian writer

"Everything is moving to small screens, but it's still all about storytelling. It all depends on how we tell the story visually for title sequence design."
Garson Yu (1961), Hong Kong-born title designer

"A great title sequence sets an expectation. You're in the theater and you see this sequence and you forget about everything else and you don't want to be anywhere else but right here at this moment and it gets you excited."
Kyle Cooper (1962), American title designer

"One of the most fun things about working on a title sequence is immersing yourself into the world of a film."
Karin Fong (1971), American title designer

"Never work with animals or children."

The young and the restless can cause quite some on-set stress, which is probably why these words of wisdom by American actor and comedian W.C. Fields (1880-1946) have resonated with both actors and directors. Having said that, cuddly animals and cute kids are also great crowd-pleasers. And so when embarking on a new cinematic adventure, you'd better decide who you want to please – the crew or the crowd – and cast accordingly.

"I could direct a dog. Kids, I don't know."
Billy Wilder (1906-2002), American writer and director

"The trick is to let them do whatever they feel like doing and play off that; you're doomed if you try to manipulate a child into doing something specific you have in mind."
Karl Malden (1912-2009), American actor

"Think twice before you write a scene with babies or infants."
Wim Wenders (1945), German director

"Never expect dogs, cats, birds or any other animals to do what you'd like them to do. Keep your shots loose."
Wim Wenders (1945), German director

"I love working with kids."
Steven Spielberg (1946), American director

"All the kids in *Bobby Fischer* were acting for the first time. They were figuring it out as we went along. It requires patience, creating situations that feel real for them, reminding them they can refer to things in their own lives for inspiration, respect and love, and lots of film."
Steven Zaillian (1953), Armenian-American screenwriter and director

Take risks

rule
10

The movie business is not one that allows for many risks or experiments. But, as Francis Ford Coppola points out, that was not always the case: "The cinema language happened by experimentation – by people not knowing what to do. But unfortunately, after 15-20 years, it became a commercial industry. People made money in the cinema, and then they began to say to the pioneers, 'Don't experiment. We want to make money. We don't want to take chances.'" Coppola calls on young filmmakers to continue taking risks, although these days that does come at a price. Coppola: "I make films. No one tells me what to do. But I make the money in the wine industry. You work another job and get up at five in the morning and write your script."

_____

"Hollywood is the only industry, even taking in soup companies, which does not have laboratories for the purpose of experimentation."
Orson Welles (1915-1985), American director

"An essential element of any art is risk. If you don't take a risk, then how are you going to make something really beautiful, that hasn't been seen before? I always like to say that cinema without risk is like having no sex and expecting to have a baby. You have to take a risk."
Francis Ford Coppola (1939), American director

"In terms of the grammar of cinema, I haven't seen anything made since the late '70s or early '80s that I felt was really pushing the ball forward... I'm frustrated by what's going on in the business, in terms of what's getting made, and I'm frustrated by my own inability to break through to something else."
Steven Soderbergh (1963), American director

"After 100 years, films should be getting really complicated. The novel has been reborn about 400 times, but it's like cinema is stuck in the birth canal."
Harmony Korine (1973), American director

Get top billing

Hollywood has a rich history when it comes to billing battles. Having your name mentioned first in the biggest and brightest letters seems of the utmost importance to some status-hungry actors and directors. When director Garson Kanin asked Spencer Tracy why, instead of letting his female co-star Katharine Hepburn come first, he insisted on top billing, Tracy replied: "This is a movie, you chowderhead, not a lifeboat!"

———————

"I honestly feel the billing situation has been a disaster to the marketing of motion pictures. You are so bound by restrictions of agents and guild requirements, you can't sell the film."
Charles M. Powell (1933-1991), Hollywood marketing executive

"I love these movies where it's just about the film. You don't have my face on the poster. It's all about the movie. I like that."
John Cusack (1966), American actor

"There was my name up in lights. I said, 'God, somebody's made a mistake!' But there it was in lights. And I sat there and said, 'Remember, you're not a star'. Yet there it was up in lights."
Marilyn Monroe (1926-1962), American actress

"It is better to be good than to be original."

rule 12

Originality is overrated. Indeed, as German-born American architect Mies van der Rohe (1886-1969), best known for his "Less is More" dictum, once said: "it is better to be good than to be original." And if making a "good" movie involves some heavy borrowing, if not downright stealing, then that's a price many a director is happy to pay.

"Self-plagiarism is style."
Alfred Hitchcock (1899-1980),
British director

"It's not where you take things from – it's where you take them to."
Jean-Luc Godard (1930),
French-Swiss director

"I steal from the best. I do it because I like to do it."
Woody Allen (1935), American
director

"I think there's no originality. I think everyone is stealing from everyone else and going back to the originals."
Ridley Scott (1937), British director

"Nothing is original. Steal from anywhere that resonates with inspiration or fuels your imagination. Devour old films, new films, music, books, paintings, photographs, poems, dreams, architecture, bridges, street signs, random conversations, trees, clouds, bodies of water, light and shadows. Select only things to steal from that speak directly to your soul. If you do this, your work (and theft) will be authentic. Authenticity is invaluable; originality is nonexistent. And don't bother concealing your thievery – celebrate it if you feel like it."
Jim Jarmusch (1953), American
director

"I steal from every movie ever made."
Quentin Tarantino (1963), American
director

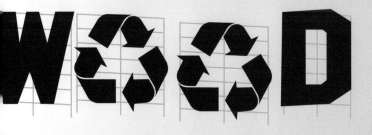

THE OLDER THE ACTRESS, THE FEWER THE PARTS

Tinseltown is no place for ageing actresses. As the years go up, most actresses find that the number of roles available to them go down. It's a sad but harsh Hollywood reality that even the great Bette Davis couldn't escape. Faced with a decline in job offers, Davis took matters into her own hands and ran an ad in Variety stating: "Mother of three – 10, 11 & 15 – divorcée. American. Thirty years experience as an actress in motion pictures. Mobile still and more affable than rumor would have it. Wants steady employment in Hollywood."

"At my age, you don't get much variety - usually some old nut who's off her track."
Katharine Hepburn (1907-2003), American actress

"I've been given great, weird, interesting parts well past my sell-by date. I remember saying to my husband when I was 38, 'Well, it's over.' And then we kicked the can down the road a little further."
Meryl Streep (1949), American actress

"My peer group was all panicked about turning 40. But I sat with an actress friend the other day who is under 30 and who makes $10 million a picture and is concerned about turning 30. So now it isn't even 40 – it's 30."
Ellen Barkin (1954), American actress

"OLD AGE IS NO PLACE FOR SISSIES."

Bette Davis (1908-1989), American actress

"Females get hired along procreative lines. After 40, we're kind of cooked."
Carrie Fisher (1956), American actress

"I remember, when I was in my late 20s and early 30s, women in their late 40s saying your career is over after 40. I thought, 'That can't be true.' They are giving up, or they are not looking, but it pretty much is true. Unless you are Meryl Streep, there are not a lot of opportunities for women in their 40s."
Melanie Griffith (1957), American actress

"They do allow you to get older in Hollywood. Some of us continue to work... It's still true: the older you get the fewer parts there are. But there are fewer movies being made overall and fewer parts for actors in general."
Michelle Pfeiffer (1958), American actress

"I'm excited about getting older – the roles are becoming more interesting. But it's hard, because I'll go up for a role that I'm the right age for and they'll want a 22-year-old. It's insane!"
Rosanna Arquette (1959), American actress

HOLLYWOOD IS SEXIST

In the early years of cinema, women played a significant role in the movie-making process, primarily as editors and actresses. Of course, these days the range of jobs available to women is much wider, from director to stunt double, but a 2012 study showed that, unfortunately, in Hollywood women are still struggling to break through the celluloid ceiling. The study, carried out by the San Diego State University Center for the Study of Women in Television and Film, showed that in 2011 only 5% of all directors were female, while they made up just 14% of all writers and an utterly depressing 4% of cinematographers.

"I'm not a person who believes in the great difference between women and men as editors. But I do think that quality is key. We're very good at organizing and discipline and patience, and patience is 50 percent of editing. You have to keep banging away at something until you get it to work. I think women are maybe better at that."
Thelma Schoonmaker (1940), American editor

45

"IF YOU HAVE A VAGINA AND AN ATTITUDE IN THIS TOWN, THEN THAT'S A LETHAL COMBINATION."

Sharon Stone (1958), American actress

"In the first twenty, thirty years of cinema large numbers of editors were women. It was considered to be a woman's job, because it was something like knitting... It was when sound came in that the men began to infiltrate the ranks of the editors because sound was somehow electrical."
Walter Murch (1943), American editor

"I think all industries are sexist in nature and I don't think the film industry is any different."
Christine Lahti (1950), American actress

"Hollywood is the definition of sexual discrimination."
Ally Sheedy (1962), American actress

"When I was doing my first movie, the only thing I knew is I wanted a female editor. I just felt a female editor would be more nurturing to the movie and to me."
Quentin Tarantino (1963), American director

"Hollywood is sexist and ageist, and that covers all the bases, I guess."
Kyra Sedgwick (1965), American actress

Have

a beginning,

a middle

and

an end

In his book *101 Things I Learned in Film School* screenwriter Neil Landau shares words of wisdom about the moviemaking métier. Amongst other things, Landau urges his readers to make sure their work has a beginning, a middle and an end. Screenwriters, directors and editors need to make sure that their efforts are directed towards "establishing and reinforcing a three-act structure." In practice this means that in act 1 you "establish the problem." In act 2 you "complicate the problem." And in act 3 you "resolve the problem."

———————

"A whole is what has a beginning and middle and end."
Aristotle (384 BC – 322 BC), Greek philosopher

"A good opening and a good ending make for a good film, provided they come close together."
Federico Fellini (1920-1993), Italian director

"A story should have a beginning, a middle and an end, but not necessarily in that order."
Jean-Luc Godard (1930), French-Swiss director

NEVER TRUST THE DIRECTOR

They're the ones who get to yell 'cut' and 'action' on set. They're the ones who will take a script by a struggling but promising screenwriter and run with it. They're the ones who create a safe environment for the delicate actor's ego or, if that doesn't work, a not-so-safe environment. As seasoned professionals will tell you: all's fair in love, war and filmmaking.

"I did whatever was necessary to get a good performance, including so-called Method acting. I made them run around the set, I scolded them, I inspired jealousy in their girlfriends... The director is a desperate beast! ... You don't deal with actors as dolls. You deal with them as people who are poets to a certain degree."
Elia Kazan (1909–2003), American director

"Filmmaking – to be a film director, you know is not a democracy; it's really a tyranny."
Woody Allen (1935), American director

"I hear stories about directors who scream at actors, or they trick them somehow to get a performance. And there are some people who try to run the whole business on fear. But I think this is such a joke – it's pathetic and stupid at the same time."
David Lynch (1946), American director

"The one big thing I know I've learned from the good directors I've worked with is this: they share an ability to approach a scene confidently and to commit to a strong visual idea, rather than just covering everything."
Steven Zaillian (1953), Armenian-American screenwriter and director

"There's the legend, and there's the facts… You know, in reality, on the set, I'm pretty crisp, pretty focused. And I don't think I necessarily inspire fear. What I like to inspire is people bringing their best game."
James Cameron (1954), Canadian director

"People think a director has to speak in that actor's language, and it's probably best for an actor; but there are so many directors that are downright destructive and negative."
Keith Gordon (1961), American actor and director

"In the moment of making a film, you're completely on your own; it's you, the camera, and the actors."
Alexander Payne (1961), American director

"I think to be a director you should probably come from another aspect of the business, because the director runs the show. If you're a writer or an actor or any part of the crew, you'll have had on-set experience, so you'll get to learn the game before you have to run the show."
Jon Favreau (1966), American actor and director

"Directing can be the greatest job in the world, but only if you let it."
Eli Roth (1972), American director

LOOKIN' GOOD, TOM!

IT'S BETTER TO BE TYPECAST THAN NOT CAST AT ALL

Sure, being typecast is annoying, but it still beats not being cast at all. Just ask any of the unemployed actors turned struggling waiters that would kill to have that 'problem.'

"After *The Wizard Of Oz* I was typecast as a lion, and there aren't all that many parts for lions."
Bert Lahr (1895-1967), American actor

"I am a typed director. If I made *Cinderella*, the audience would immediately be looking for a body in the coach."
Alfred Hitchcock (1899-1980), British director

"I've made so many movies playing a hooker that they don't pay me in the regular way anymore. They leave it on the dresser"
Shirley MacLaine (1934), American actress

"I always believe in casting into who somebody is in real life and not asking them to play-act or to be somebody else."
Tony Scott (1944), English director

"The good thing about getting older is that when they do cast you it's often something interesting – you're no longer asked to be the beautiful leading lady."
Meryl Streep (1949), American actress

"Leia follows me like a vague smell."
Carrie Fisher (1956), American actress

"I could play 5000 drug addicts and I'd still be known as Mrs. Corset Queen."
Helena Bonham Carter (1966), British actress

SID VICIOUS

ROSENCRANTZ

LEE HARVEY OSWALD

DRACULA

DREXL SPIVEY

STANSFIELD

BEETHOVEN

REV. DIMMESDALE

ZORG

IVAN KORSHUNOV

DR. SMITH

SHELLY RUNYON

BUFORD DILL

MASON VERGER

O.W. GRANT

DEVIL

ROLFE

SIRIUS BLACK

JIM GORDON

FATHER SOLOMON

GARY OLDMAN

"COMPLETE NUDITY IS NEVER PERMITTED."

rule
18

Sex, violence and crime are recurring themes in many a movie, but in 1930 the Motion Picture Producers and Distributors of America (MPPDA) laid down the law, so to speak, in the Motion Picture Production Code. Also known as the Hays Code – after the MPPDA's first president and chief movie censor of the time, Will H. Hays – it served as a moral guideline, stating what was and more importantly, what was not permissible on the silver screen. Complete nudity was never permitted, "brutal killings" were "not to be presented in detail" and "dances suggesting or representing sexual actions or indecent passion" were simply "forbidden." The Production Code was officially laid to rest in the late sixties and was eventually replaced by the rating system.

———

"Good taste is good business."
Will H. Hays (1879-1954), American movie censor

"What critics call dirty in our movies, they call lusty in foreign films."
Billy Wilder (1906-2002), American writer and director

PULP FICTION

57

a QUENTIN TARANTINO film

Starring Bruce Willis · John Travolta · Samuel L. Jackson **Co-Starring** Amanda Plummer
Duane Whitaker · Eric Stoltz · Frank Whaley · Maria de Medeiros · Paul Calderon · Peter Greene
Phil LaMarr · Rosanna Arquette · Tim Roth · Uma Thurman · Ving Rhames **Directed by** Quentin Tarantino
Screenplay by Quentin Tarantino **Stories** Roger Avary **A Band Apart**

SE7EN

a DAVID FINCHER film

Starring Brad Pitt · Morgan Freeman **Co-Starring** Andrew Kevin Walker · Bob Collins · Bob Mack
Daniel Zacapa · Endre Hules · George Christy · Gwyneth Paltrow · Hawthorne James · John Cassini
Peter Crombie · R. Lee Ermey · Reg E. Cathey · William Davidson **Directed by** David Fincher
Written By Andrew Kevin Walker New Line Cinema

"G means the hero gets the girl. R means the villain gets the girl. X means everybody gets the girl."
Kirk Douglas (1916), American actor

"The trouble with censors is that they worry if a girl has cleavage. They ought to worry if she hasn't any."
Marilyn Monroe (1926-1962), American actress

"Sanitized violence in movies has been accepted for years. What seems to upset everybody now is the showing of the consequences of violence."
Stanley Kubrick (1928-1999), American director

"When [Elizabeth Taylor] and I were young, those were the glory days of Hollywood, when movies were about characters, stories, acting and scripts... movies that didn't include actors doing drugs openly and actors being maniacal."
Shirley MacLaine (1934), American actress

"There is a fine line between censorship and good taste and moral responsibility."
Steven Spielberg (1946), American director

"The rating system is completely screwed up. It has to be redone. It's crazy, it's totally crazy. Do you know how many people, innocent people, were mowed down in *Road to Perdition*? And that got an R. You can see Maria Bello's pubic hair in *The Cooler* and it got an NC-17. Somebody's gotta stand up and say pubic hair is good, murder is bad. Sex is good, violence is bad."
William Macy (1950), American actor

"Sure, *Kill Bill*'s a violent movie. But it's a Tarantino movie. You don't go to see Metallica and ask the fuckers to turn the music down."
Quentin Tarantino (1963), American director

"When I was a child, the temptation to sin was always a romantic option. This romantic option lead me to the cinema, a place where sin was welcome."
Harmony Korine (1973), American director

Bring magic to the silver screen

From the 17th-century magic lanterns and 19th-century illusion toys to Edison's Kinetoscope and the Lumière brothers' Cinématographe, right down to their modern equivalents: the history of film and moving image has always been about creating illusions and magic. It's hardly surprising then that in the late 1900s it was magicians who were one of the first to incorporate moving images in their performance. Continue the legacy and make sure you bring magic to the silver screen.

rule
19

"A film is a ribbon of dreams. The camera is much more than a recording apparatus; it is a medium via which messages reach us from another world that is not ours and that brings us to the heart of a great secret. Here magic begins."
Orson Welles (1915-1985), American director

"The screen is a magic medium. It has such power that it can retain interest as it conveys emotions and moods that no other art form can hope to tackle."
Stanley Kubrick (1928-1999), American director

"I think cinema, movies, and magic have always been closely associated. The very earliest people who made films were magicians."
Francis Ford Coppola (1939), American director

"Cinema is its own language. And with it you can say so many things, because you've got time and sequences. You've got dialogue. You've got music. You've got sound effects. You have so many tools. And so you can express a feeling and a thought that can't be conveyed any other way. It's a magical medium."
David Lynch (1946), American director

"Film to me is a magical medium that makes you dream... allows you to dream in the dark. It's just a fantastic thing, to get lost inside the world of film."
David Lynch (1946), American director

"There's magic to editing. The magic is the discovery of something new that wasn't intended that works for the movie."
Michael Tronick (1949), American editor

"Grab 'em by the throat and never let 'em go."

Legendary writer and director Billy Wilder composed a list of 10 screenwriting tips, which included: "Grab 'em by the throat and never let 'em go." So make them laugh. Make them cry. Scare the living daylights out of them. Entertain your public from start to finish.

"The Wilder message is don't bore - don't bore people."
Billy Wilder (1906-2002),
American writer and director

"The audience goes to sleep really quickly! If you have a slight pause at the wrong time, that's it!"
Woody Allen (1935), American
director

"I don't walk out of movies. It's too hard to make a movie – I know how hard it is – so I don't walk out of a movie I've paid to see. I'd rather sit there and be bored."
Gary Winick (1961-2011),
American director

"I think it's a lot more fun to take the audience to a place where they really don't know what's going to happen; anything can still occur right up until the last frame."
Bryan Singer (1965), American
director

"I generally don't walk out of films. If I start a book and I don't love it by page 100, I will stop reading because it's just too much of a time commitment. But you never know with a movie what's going to turn around."
David Dobkin (1969), American
director

THERE IS A METHOD TO THE MADNESS

rule 21

Method acting, based on the teachings of the Russian director Constantin Stanislavski and popularized by the American director Lee Strasberg, remains a rather controversial acting technique. It has been adopted by some of the most critically-acclaimed actors in Western cinema – Brando, Dean and Pacino to name but a few – but has also been ridiculed by opponents. Contrary to popular belief, Method acting does not involve an actor 'becoming' the character or 'staying' in character once the cameras stop rolling.

"Never lose yourself on stage. Always act in your own person, as an artist. You can never get away from yourself. The moment you lose yourself on the stage marks the departure from truly living your part and the beginning of exaggerated false acting... Always and forever, when you are on the stage, you must play yourself."
Constantin Stanislavski (1863-1938), Russian actor and director

"Method acting? There are quite a few methods. Mine involves a lot of talent, a glass and some cracked ice."
John Barrymore (1882-1942), American actor

"Method acting is what all actors have always done whenever they acted well."
Lee Strasberg (1901-1982), American actor and director

"[Method actors] act from the inside out. They communicate emotions they really feel. They give you a sense of life."
Tennessee Williams (1911-1983), American playwright

"Lee Strasberg ruined an entire generation of actors with that sense memory crap."
Arthur Penn (1922-2010), American director

"The idea is, you learn to use everything that happened in your life and you learn to use it in creating the character you're working on. You learn to dig into your unconscious and make use of every experience you ever had."
Marlon Brando (1924-2004), American actor

"I was talking to Sean Penn on the phone today. I told him it was interesting that they managed to leave me off this long list of Method actors they'd published in some article. I told him, 'I'm still fooling them!' I consider it an accomplishment. Because there's probably no one who understands Method acting better academically than I do, or actually uses it more in his work."
Jack Nicholson (1937), American actor

"I don't believe in Method acting, where you walk around in character all the time. I still retain a part of myself when I come home and I still talk to my dog the same way."
Kelly McGillis (1957), American actress

"I despise those prick actors who say, 'I was in character,' and 'I became the character,' and all that stuff. It's hideous. It's just masturbation at the highest level."
Johnny Depp (1963), American actor

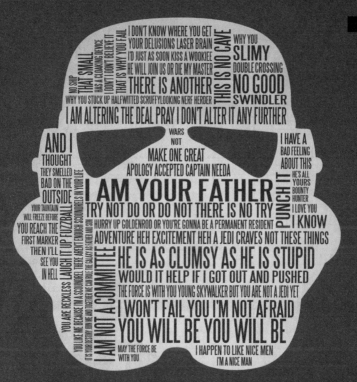

STAR WARS EPISODE V

THE EMPIRE STRIKES BACK
A GEORGE LUCAS FILM

"Nobody ever put up a statue to a critic."

Don't bother playing to the crowd or pleasing the critics. It's like the Finnish composer Jean Sibelius (1865-1957) said: "Pay no attention to what the critics say. A statue has never been erected in honor of a critic."

"I'm not interested in pleasing the critics. I`ll take my chances pleasing the audiences."
Walt Disney (1901-1966), American producer

"No critic writing about a film could say more than the film itself, although they do their best to make us think the opposite."
Federico Fellini (1920-1993), Italian director

"From the very beginning, all of my films have divided the critics. Some have thought them wonderful, and others have found very little good to say. But subsequent critical opinion has always resulted in a very remarkable shift to the favorable."
Stanley Kubrick (1928-1999), American director

"Some day I'll make a film that critics will like. When I have money to waste."
François Truffaut (1932-1984), French film critic and director

"If a film gets bad reviews, nobody comes. If a film gets good reviews, maybe people come, and maybe nobody comes. But it's never, if it gets good reviews, then they really come. For me, it's lose, and, you know... maybe."
Woody Allen (1935), American director

"I don't spend sleepless nights over getting very bad reviews."
Werner Herzog (1942) German director

"You can't help but be affected when you read the reviews. I try not to take it too seriously one way or the other... I think you have your perspective at all times; perspective meaning that you're in it for the long haul."
John Carpenter (1948), American director

"Nothing to me is unexpected. No disappointment is unexpected – whether it's movies or people or relationships. I'm always ready for the punch directly between the eyes."
Brian Grazer (1951), American producer

"I keep asking myself: 'Why do I care?' I know that my work is a result of 110 percent effort. I know how I feel about the film. Why do I care about reviews? Why do I care about the box office? But as soon as I ask the question, a voice in the back of my head always answers: 'Because you have to care.' You can't live without caring. That's who you are, and therefore you must suffer from time to time."
Ron Howard (1954), American actor and director

"My favorite review described me as the cinematic equivalent of junk mail."
Steve Buscemi (1957), American actor

"I feel reviewers are tougher on comedies in general. They don't take them seriously, and the ones that get great reviews are not necessarily the ones that I like. I just feel I'm on a different page from the reviewers, so I've learned not to care about them too much."
Bobby Farrelly (1958), American director

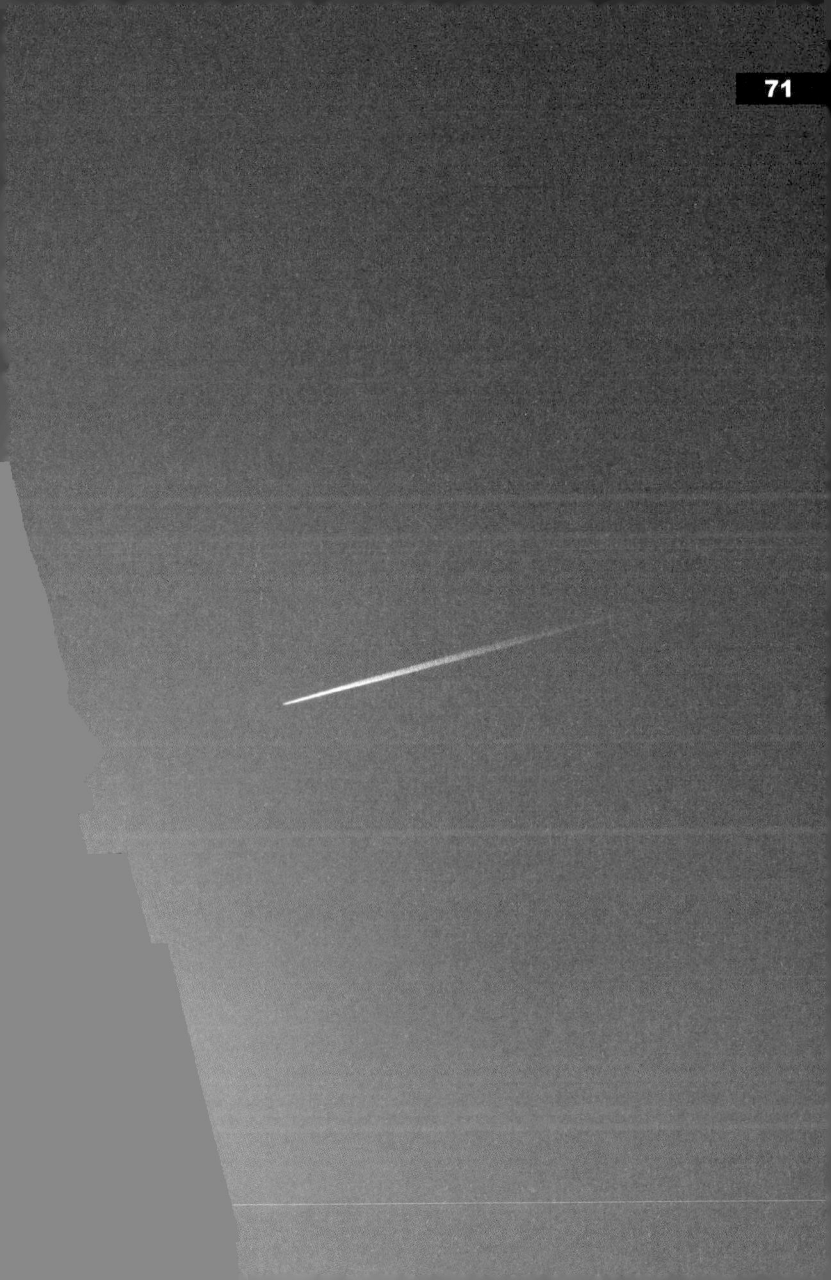

Make movies for planet earth

When he appeared on American talk show *The View*, Quentin Tarantino was asked about the amount of violence in *Kill Bill*. He shot back with one brilliant one-liner. "Barbara Walters was asking me about the blood and stuff, and I said, 'Well, you know, that's a staple of Japanese cinema.' And then she came back: 'But this is America.' And I go: 'I don't make movies for America. I make movies for planet Earth.'" We live in a globalized world: make movies for planet earth.

"I don't consider myself qualified to do a movie about international intrigue – I seldom leave the country."
John Hughes (1950), American director

"As the business has internationalized, more and more focus has gone on dumbing down the movies, if you will. They're much more interested in films that translate into multi-continents like action, sex, big stars."
Alan Shapiro (1957), American director

"I am not an American filmmaker. I make movies for planet Earth."
Quentin Tarantino (1963), American director

KILL BILL VOLUME 1

A QUENTIN TARANTINO FILM

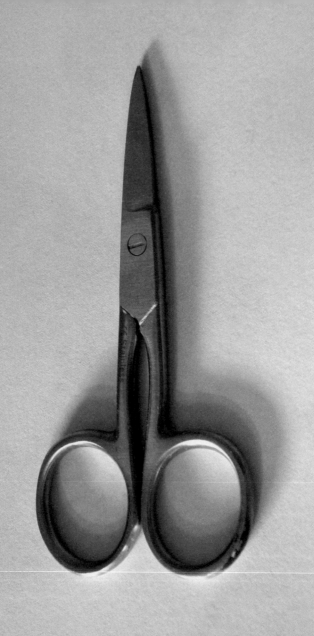

"Let other people cut your trailer!"

rule 24

In 2006 the magazine *MovieMaker* published German director Wim Wenders' Golden Rules. All 50 of them. Rule number 23? "Let other people cut your trailer!" Why? Because when you've invested so much time and energy in a project, it's hard to find that perfect balance between creating a trailer that teases to one that leaves little to nothing to the audience's imagination.

———

"We did all kinds of things in trailers to help sell films. We had a famous exploding helicopter shot from one of those Filipino productions that we'd cut in every time a trailer was too dull because that was always exciting."
Joe Dante (1946), American director

"When you are running at full speed to complete your film on your way to your premiere, don't fool yourself that you have the perspective to cut your own trailer."
Tiffany Shlain (1970), American director

DON'T ANSWER THE PHONE

If 1980s horror flicks have taught trembling audiences one thing, it is that you should never, ever answer the phone. It has become something of a Hollywood cliché, immortalized in movies as diverse as *Scream* (with the cheerful tagline "Don't Answer The Phone. Don't Open The Door. Don't Try To Escape."), and *Memento* (who could forget Leonard discovering his tattoo while one the phone?) to the classic horror movie *Don't answer the Phone* (with a trailer offering the following advice: "Run if you can. Scream if you are able. But whatever you do, don't answer the phone!").

――――――――

"Horror films don't create fear. They release it."
Wes Craven (1939), American director

"What scares me is what scares you. We're all afraid of the same things. That's why horror is such a powerful genre. All you have to do is ask yourself what frightens you and you'll know what frightens me."
John Carpenter (1948), American director

"Never answer the phone in a horror movie. To avoid disaster, text."
Joe Queenan (1950), American critic and author

SEX SELLS

rule
26

In 2010 Tim Walker, a features writer for *The Independent*, wrote an article in which he convincingly argued that sex no longer sells movies. Where once a "mere glimpse of Demi Moore's jugs could garner $266m in takings," times have changed. Walker: "The internet has provided us with free access to many things we previously expected to pay good money for, including pictures of movie stars' breasts."

———

"Part of the appeal historically of seeing one of your favorite actors naked or having sex on screen was that it was rare. Today, you can trip over a crack in the sidewalk and stumble upon sexual content. It's not special any more, and so it doesn't draw you into the movie theatre."
Jay Fernandez, The Hollywood Reporter

"Sex is boring unless you're doing it."
Ridley Scott (1937), British director

"Not enough sex – I've never heard that from a studio."
Paul Verhoeven (1938), Dutch director

Have a realistic budget

Making movies is an expensive undertaking. There's sets, costumes, trailers, crew, catering, overpaid actors, you name it. The somewhat ambiguous but apparently highly coveted title of "most expensive movie ever made" has been bestowed on several movies, but when adjusted for inflation, the award goes to *Cleopatra*. Released in 1963, this epic movie starring Elizabeth Taylor and Richard Burton had a budget of $ 44 million. It took years before the movie made its money back.

"I work on a small budget. I have always had the money before I wrote the script. So when I pull the script out of the typewriter, the next day I give it to my production people and we go into production with it. Whereas some other person writes a perfectly wonderful script, and then they've got to raise $30, 40 million to make the film."
Woody Allen (1935), American director

"The more money you have the more you can do with it, sure. But the less you can say with it."
Wim Wenders (1945), German director

"When you're in front of the camera, for a small budget or a big budget movie, there's no difference."
Monica Bellucci (1964), Italian actress

"That's the biggest rule in Hollywood: Don't spend your own money."
Pauly Shore (1968), American actor

Secure final cut

Securing final cut is easier said than done. Much to their chagrin, directors, even award-winning ones, aren't always given creative control of the movie they've directed. It's their bankability, and in a few cases their reputation, that helps seal the deal.

———

"I have ten commandments. The first nine are, thou shalt not bore. The tenth is, thou shalt have right of final cut."
Billy Wilder (1906-2002), American writer and director

"Final cut is overrated. Only fools keep insisting on always having the final word. The wise swallow their pride in order to get to the best possible cut."
Wim Wenders (1945), German director

"When I made *Dune*, I didn't have final cut. It was a huge, huge sadness, because I felt I had sold out, and on top of that, the film was a failure at the box office. If you do what you believe in and have a failure, that's one thing; you can still live with yourself. But if you don't, it's like dying twice. It's very, very painful."
David Lynch (1946), American director

"In some circumstances I've had less control than I've had in others. Usually, I've just been very lucky. That, and I've tried to stick to my guns as much as possible. In a few cases, I wasn't so lucky, but that's the toughest battle a director has."
John Carpenter (1948), American director

"Don't let the fuckers get ya. They can either help you, or not help you, but they can't stop you. People who finance films, distribute films, promote films and exhibit films are not filmmakers. They are not interested in letting filmmakers define and dictate the way they do their business, so filmmakers should have no interest in allowing them to dictate the way a film is made. Carry a gun if necessary."
Jim Jarmusch (1953), American director

NERD

INFO

"Filmmaking is a collaborative process."

rule 29

Your name might be the biggest on the marquee but never forget that filmmaking is a joint effort. Give credit where credit's due and be kind to the crew or be prepared to suffer the consequences.

"Most actors learn very early on that the editor is the one to make friends with because their performance depends a great deal on the editor, and the taste and talent of the editor."
George Lucas (1944), American director

"Filmmaking is a collaborative process... But treat all collaborators as equals and with respect. A production assistant who is holding back traffic so the crew can get a shot is no less important than the actors in the scene, the director of photography, the production designer or the director. Hierarchy is for those whose egos are inflated or out of control, or for people in the military."
Jim Jarmusch (1953), American director

"My heroes are the camera crew and the electricians. They work such long hours."
Adam Baldwin (1962), American actor

"More than anything as I get older, it's really about the company I keep. [Making a film] takes you away from your family for months. So it had better be with people you respect, and it better be something that means something to you."
Brad Pitt (1963), American actor

"Don't ever fuck with the crew. However the coffee comes, I drink it. If it's black, too bad."
John Leguizamo (1964), Colombian-American actor

"The crew are the faces you see every morning and last at night before you go home. I spend more time with those people than I do with my friends and family, so they're forever a part of you and who you become as an actor so I hope I see them again."
Claudia Black (1972), Australian actress

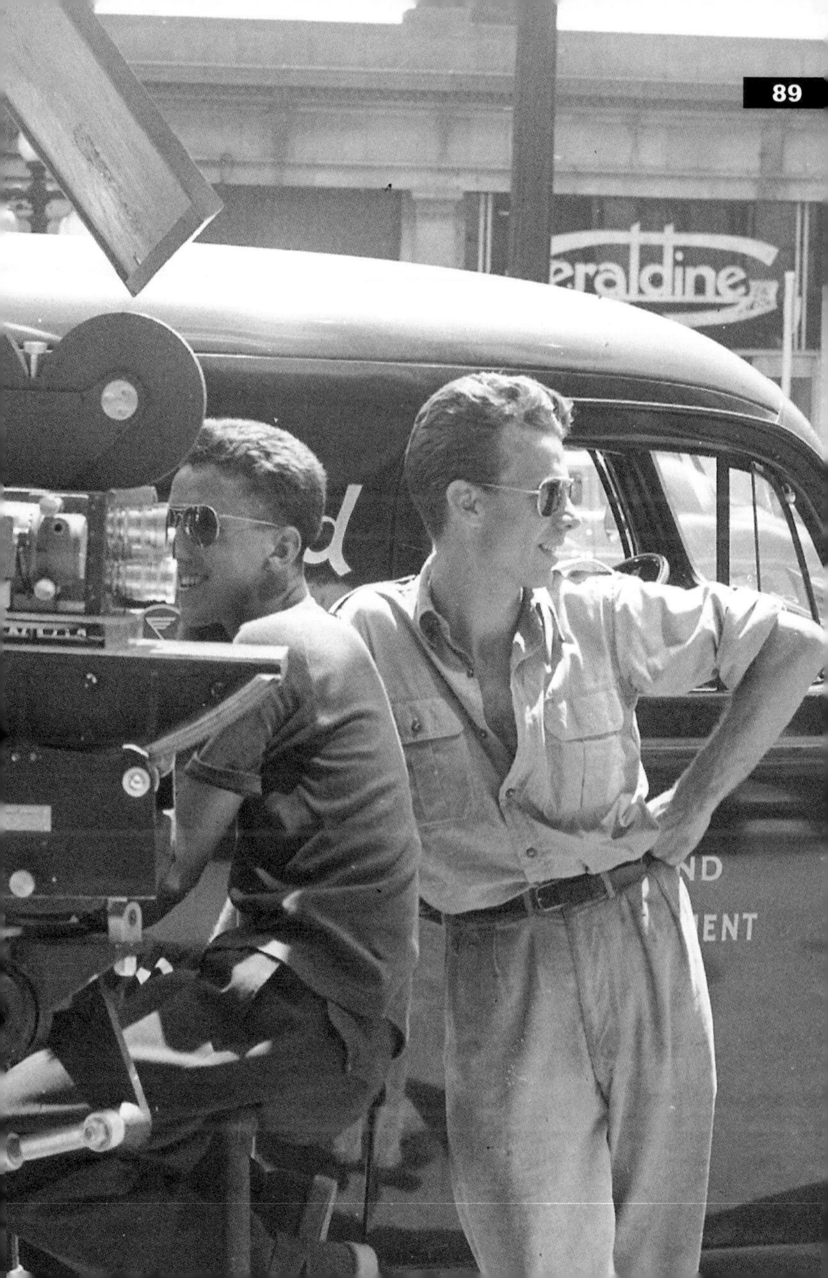
eraldine
ND
MENT

"Suffering is more cinematic than happiness."

rule 30

As one of the exponents of the so-called 'cinema of moral anxiety,' Polish director Krzysztof Kieslowski, who started his career in documentary filmmaking, summed up the intrinsic dramatic nature of cinema by stating that "suffering is more cinematic than happiness."

"I would never write about someone who is not at the end of his rope."
Stanley Elkin (1930-1995), American novelist

"If my film makes one more person miserable, I'll feel I've done my job."

Woody Allen (1935), American director

"All of us seem to be playing roles in real-life dramas that we are not only starring in but have been scripting, too. We are each the author and leading player in the entertainment called 'My Life'."
Shirley MacLaine (1934), American actress

"People love seeing violence and horrible things. The human being is bad and he can't stand more than five minutes of happiness. Put him in a dark theater and ask him to look at two hours of happiness and he'd walk out or fall asleep."
Paul Verhoeven (1938), Dutch director

Film is emotion

It's a blow in the face of all those Film Studies graduates, but at the end of the day film deals with emotion, not intellect. In the words of German director Werner Herzog: "Film should be looked at straight on, it is not the art of scholars but of illiterates."

"I would say that there is no art form that has so much in common with film as music. Both affect our emotions directly, not via the intellect."
Ingmar Bergman (1918-2007),
Swedish director

"No form of art goes beyond ordinary consciousness as film does, straight to our emotions, deep into the twilight room of the soul."
Ingmar Bergman (1918-2007),
Swedish director

"I look at film as closer to a painting or a piece of music; it's an impression... an impression of character and total atmosphere... The attempt is to enlist an audience emotionally, not intellectually."
Robert Altman (1925-2006),
American director

"I don't think you should feel about a film. You should feel about a woman, not a movie. You can't kiss a movie."
Jean-Luc Godard (1930),
French-Swiss director

"Film is not analysis, it is the agitation of mind; cinema comes from the country fair and the circus, not from art and academicism."
Werner Herzog (1942), German
director

HERZOG

HAVE A HAPPY ENDING

rule 32

In a 2009 BBC article Finlo Rohrer addresses the general public's alleged preference for movies with a happy ending. According to Rohrer the process of "happyendingification" dates back to the 1930s, the time of the Great Depression, when audiences on "both sides of the Atlantic" were in dire need of "a dose of escapist fun" or "so the financiers of culture thought." The Hollywood happy ending was born and as a consequence novels and fairy tales that were brought to the big screen now got a "happily ever after."

"If you want a happy ending, that depends, of course, on where you stop your story."
Orson Welles (1915-1985), American director

"It's no surprise to say that American movies specialize in stories of accomplishment. When Jennifer Grey finally dares to make the scary leap at the end of *Dirty Dancing*, when the Karate Kid performs the impossible kick that wipes out his opponent, or when King George VI gets through his wartime speech without stammering – those accomplishments are among the great pleasures of cinema."
Lindsay Doran, American producer

"Audiences don't care about an accomplishment unless it's shared with someone else. What makes an audience happy is not the moment of victory but the moment afterwards when the winners share that victory with someone they love."
Marty Seligman (1942), American psychologist

"Continuity is overrated."

rule 33

A glass that goes from being half full to completely empty. A corsage that changes from the left to right wrist in the blink of an eye. Or Judy Garland's pigtails in *The Wizard of Oz* that are a different length almost every other scene. Continuity mistakes, although often overlooked by script supervisors, are seldom missed by the ever-growing online community of film freaks who seem to enjoy nothing more than listing the errors on blogs, dedicated sites and of course the IMDb.

"Your continuity girl is always right about screen directions, jumping the axis and that sort of stuff. Don't fight her. Bring her flowers."
Wim Wenders (1945), German director

"Always remember: Continuity is overrated!"
Wim Wenders (1945), German director

"Everyone's got VCRs and DVDs where they can go back and watch these things so closely. You have to be very careful making a movie now because people can watch them a hundred times. In 1986 you'd make a film and people would watch it once or twice. You'd think, 'They're not gonna catch this.'"
Mark L. Lester (1946), American director

"Every other art form is largely about continuity; film is largely about discontinuity."
Anthony Minghella (1954-2008), English director

"Working for Kubrick I learned what a perfectionist really is. During the scenes in the barracks I had to make sure the beds were a certain distance apart from each other and from the walls so that they were in exactly the same spot each time we walked onto the set, down to the last tenth of an inch!"
Julie Ann Robinson Lyman (1959), English script supervisor

"In my experience, the best mistake spotters are people who love watching movies and [they] develop such an eye for it that they'll pick up on most mistakes even in casual viewing. It's not really faultfinding, just another way they enjoy the films."
Jon Sandys (1979), English author of Movie Mistakes

"Editors spot continuity errors long before the naive viewer. Hell, those of us who still edit material shot on film spot a speck of dirt covering 1/1000 of the frame for 1/24 of a second as the film is being projected. Here's why, in my opinion, you see a lack of literal continuity in film: Editors, working with their directors, always look for the great moments – those that must be in the film lest we short-change the audience. Often, the road from one great moment to the next (that is, a great moment in the next shot) is bumpy in terms of continuity."
Michael R. Miller, American editor

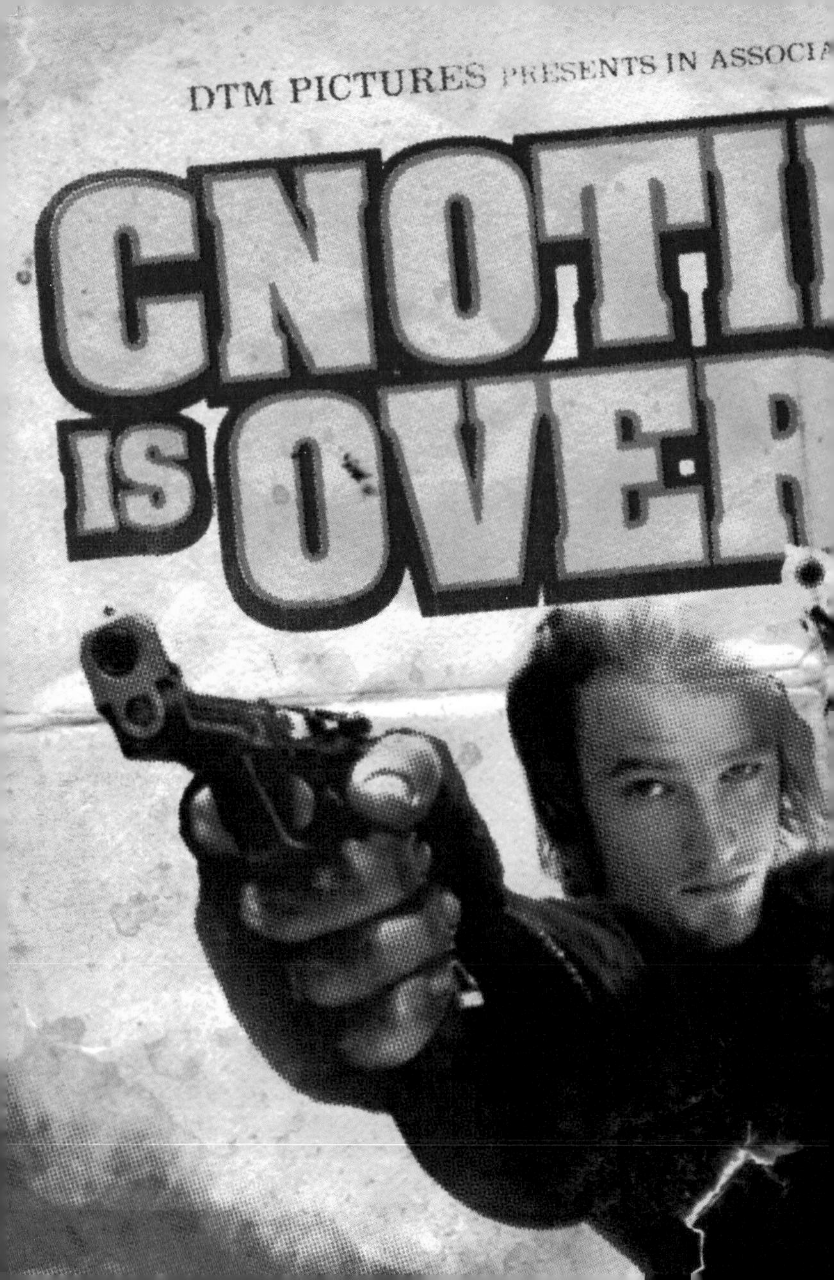
DTM PICTURES PRESENTS IN ASSOCIA
CNOT
IS OVER

WITH PAPERDOLL WRITING

UYTI
RATED

A MARTY DIBERGI FILM

"THE BASTARD SO
OF MEMENTO AND
PULP FICTION"

★★★★
EMPIRE MAGAZINE

rule 34

SHOOT EVERY SHOT

This rule is open to multiple interpretations. To some directors, shooting every shot means that they themselves need to physically shoot every single shot. To others it simply means shooting every single shot you can in order to avoid those expensive additional shooting days.

———

"If you look at guys who are not lazy, let's say Steven Spielberg, or something – you know, they work. They go out on location somewhere, and they live in the desert for a year, or in some godforsaken country for ages, making a film. And they shoot every angle and do everything. I can't do that. I don't have the patience."
Woody Allen (1935), American director

"I think there's only one or two films where I've had all the financial support I needed. All the rest, I wish I'd had the money to shoot another ten days."
Martin Scorsese (1942), American director

"Shoot every shot... This is not to say that a second unit director wouldn't shoot it better, but doing it yourself keeps the tone consistent."
Zack Snyder (1966), American actor, film director

"Thou shalt shoot every shot twice…"
The Guerilla Film Makers Handbook

Know your lines

Be on time. Know your lines.
Sounds easy enough. But apparently
is extremely hard. How else could
you explain the ever-present stories
about rambling actresses and
notoriously late actors?

"There was an actress named
Marilyn Monroe. She was always late.
She never remembered her lines. She
was a pain in the ass. My Aunt Millie
is a nice lady. If she were in pictures,
she would always be on time. She
would know her lines. She would be
nice. Why does everyone in Hollywood
want to work with Marilyn Monroe and
no one wants to work with my Aunt
Millie. Because no one will go to the
movies to watch my Aunt Millie."
*Billy Wilder (1906-2002), American
writer and director*

"Come to work on time, know your lines and don't bump into the other actors."

Spencer Tracy (1900-1967), American actor

"I've got no problem if people want to spend hours beforehand preparing before they come on-set, as long as they don't keep you waiting. And I've read Stanislavski and did the Method myself, and all that, but now I've simplified it: learn your lines, show up, and get on with it."
Anthony Hopkins (1937), Welsh actor

"Smart money is learn the lines. Just learn the whole script before you start shooting. That makes shooting a joy."
William Macy (1950), American actor

"I now have a gigantic amount of sympathy for all the directors I've ever worked with. I wish to issue a retroactive apology for every time I was even 30 seconds late to the set."
Ben Affleck (1972), American actor

What happens on set, stays on set

A movie set is like Vegas: what happens on set, stays on set. From on-set romances to a leading man's meltdown...

"All love scenes started on the set are continued in the dressing room."
Alfred Hitchcock (1899-1980), British director

"I had quite a relationship with Robert Mitchum. And Yves Montand... I was attracted to some of the directors... and everyone knows that what happened on a set stayed on a set. No one talked."
Shirley MacLaine (1934), American actress

"A star on a movie set is like a time bomb. That bomb has got to be defused so people can approach it without fear."
Jack Nicholson (1937), American actor

"Difficult? Me? I don't think I am difficult compared to other people. It is hard to make a movie at the best of times, so you don't want to give people a hard time. People all have their own agendas. But it is not worth acting out something from your own history to make a point on a film set. If you have a problem with, say, your father or some other father figure, why give the director a tough time?"
Robert De Niro (1943), American actor

"Actors can be difficult, so that's why directors speak to other directors that have worked with that person before, so you can find out for sure – background checks. I'm serious."
Spike Lee (1957), American director

CUT
ON
MOTION

rule
37

In his book *On Film Editing* (1984) American director Edward Dmytryk (1908-1999) introduced his "rules of cutting." Rule number 3 dictates that: "Whenever possible, cut 'in movement'." According to Dmytryk the so-called "action cut" is the "first bit of cutting lore learned by every apprentice." Dmytryk: "The cutter should look for some movement of the actor who holds the viewer's attention and use that movement to trigger the cut from one scene to the next."

"When I was a neophyte editor, I defended a cut by saying I had 'cut on motion.' Andrei Konchalovsky, who had challenged the cut, said in his charming Russian accent, 'Don't cut on motion, cut on emotion.'"
Michael R. Miller, American editor

"There is a cause and effect relationship between cuts. One cut has to lead into the next and the next and resonate back and forth so they fit."
Michael Kahn (1935), American editor

FRANCIS'
ESSENCE

rule
38

Editing

'The Essence of Cinema'

American director Francis Ford Coppola has called editing "the essence of cinema," because it's "the combination of what can be extraordinary images of people during emotional moments, or images in a general sense, put together in a kind of alchemy."

"Good editing makes a film look well-directed. Great editing makes a film look like it wasn't directed at all."
Victor Fleming (1889-1949), American director

"I love editing. I think I like it more than any other phase of filmmaking. If I wanted to be frivolous, I might say that everything that precedes editing is merely a way of producing film to edit."
Stanley Kubrick (1928-1999), American director

"Editing is the transformation of chance into destiny."
Jean-Luc Godard (1930), French-Swiss director

"Editing is the only process. The shooting is the pleasant work. The editing makes the movie, so I spend all my life in editing."
Garry Marshall (1934), American director

"When we go from that room into this room, with the first cut of the picture, and put it up on the screen for the first time, it's always like a cold shower. And all your grandiose ambitions reduce themselves to: How can I save this from being an embarrassment?"
Woody Allen (1935), American director

"Film editing is now something almost everyone can do at a simple level and enjoy it, but to take it to a higher level requires the same dedication and persistence that any art form does."
Walter Murch (1943), American editor

"Editing can take a bad performance and make it seem passable, but the nuances of a great performance have to be there intact."
Mark Romanek (1959), American director

Schedule a test screening

You've spent days, weeks or even months on the set and in the editing room. You know the material inside and out, which is exactly why you need a fresh pair of eyes to look at your movie before it is released.

"When I finish a film completely, there's about a half dozen, maybe eight people, that I do want to see the movie. I will invite Diane Keaton here. I will invite some personal friends of mine, between six and 10, maximum. And once they've seen the picture, I don't much care anymore."
Woody Allen (1935), American director

"The whole process of making movies and writing screenplays is visceral and intuitive. When you actually go to a preview you're asking 600 people, who come from different demographics, to become Siskel and Ebert by the end of the evening. It's absolutely rubbish."
Ridley Scott (1937), British director

"Although you can't make a film with the audience in mind, at a certain point, before it's finished, you need to experience the film with a group. Sometimes you lose your objectivity a little, and you need to get a feel for what's working and what isn't."
David Lynch (1946), American director

"What I like about test screenings is the reaction you get from the audience, more so than the cards and the statistics they give you at the end."
Spike Lee (1957), American director

"We test our movies extensively. I'm always there myself. It's sometimes difficult to sit through, especially if it's a version of the movie that's not working particularly well. You have to absorb the pain so that when you get back in the editing room you can (I'll say this in quotation marks) 'Cut your little darlings.'"
Bobby Farrelly (1958), American director

"If I made a drama, I could understand not testing it because you're not looking for that visceral audience response. People are supposed to sit there and absorb a drama, so it's hard to tell whether it's working or not, anyway. Comedy's much different, so I find the testing process crucial."
Todd Philips (1970), American director

Slow-in and slow-out

Animators Frank Thomas and Ollie Johnston spent the majority of their working life at the Walt Disney Studios. After they retired, the two members of Disney's orginal *Nine Old Men* wrote the book *Illusion Of Life.* Often referred to as the Bible of Animation, the book contains the 12 basic principles of animation:

1. Squash and stretch
2. Anticipation
3. Staging
4. Straight Ahead Action and Pose to Pose
5. Follow Through and Overlapping Action
6. Slow-In and Slow-Out
7. Arcs
8. Secondary Action
9. Timing
10. Exaggeration
11. Solid Drawing (same or different as Weight)
12. Appeal

"Cartoonists have the best casting system. If they don't like an actor, they just tear him up."

Alfred Hitchcock (1899-1980), British director

"Animation can explain whatever the mind of man can conceive."
Walt Disney (1901-1966), American producer

"Fewer drawings make the action faster and more drawings make the action slower. Slow-ins and slow-outs soften the action, making it more life-like. For a gag action, we may omit some slow-out or slow-ins for shock appeal or the surprise element. This will give more snap to the scene."
Frank Thomas (1912-2004) and Ollie Johnston (1912-2008), American animators

"Compared to animation, live action is easy. It doesn't take nearly as long to make live action films, either. My good friend Marty Scorsese used to make two-and-a-half films to my one! Plus, they pay live directors more. Not only is it easier, they pay the bastards more!"
Ralph Bakshi (1938), Israeli-American director

MAKE AN ENTRANCE

rule 41

Make sure your main characters make an entrance. And while you're at it: make it a memorable one. Think naked Schwarzenegger curled up in the fetal position in *The Terminator*. Or actress Ursula Andress, who, dressed in her white bikini, emerged from the sea in *Dr No*. An iconic movie entrance, mimicked years later by Halle Berry in another Bond movie, *Die Another Day*.

———

"An actor entering through the door, you've got nothing. But if he enters through the window, you've got a story."
Billy Wilder (1906-2002), American writer and director

"My entrance in the film wearing the bikini on that beautiful beach made me world-famous as 'the Bond girl'."
Ursula Andress (1936), Swiss actress

"We were paying homage to Ursula Andress. They wanted me to come out and do what she did. It was a little daunting, because she did it so well, and it's a big moment in film history and in Bond history."
Halle Berry, (1966), American actress

Movie-making is a BUSINESS

rule
42

Make no mistake about it: moviemaking is a business. That's why they call it show business.

———————

"It's called show business, not show art."
Jean Seberg (1938-1979), American actress

"With genre films that do well, you can just bet that there are twenty-six or one hundred versions of *Blair Witch* in the works, and they're going to be done by everybody with no real impulse to do it except that it made so much money and they want to be on that gravy train."
Wes Craven (1939), American director

"Most people are interested in the business out there. It comes down to the weekly totals, the grosses, per-screen averages, and all that shit. It's a place where bad films become good films if they make a lot of money, and vice versa. That's a real sticky trap to get into."
Richard Linklater (1960), American director

"Just because you've made a couple movies, you've done some good movies, you've been nominated for some Academy Awards, whatever, nobody's entitled. It's a business. If they don't see it, I can think they're wrong, but I'm not entitled to a $15 million budget to make a film."
Edward Norton (1969), American actor and director

What if nothing exists and we're all in somebody's dream? | Woody Allen

It's all about the money

In a 2004 interview with *The Observer* Woody Allen lamented the fact that the studio system, once considered a relic of Hollywood's past, was back in full force: "Studios are back in command and are not that interested in pictures that make only a little bit of money. When I was younger, every week we'd get a Fellini or a Bergman or a Godard or Truffaut, but now you almost never get any of that. Filmmakers like myself have a hard time. The avaricious studios couldn't care less about good films – if they get a good film they're twice as happy, but money-making films are their goal. They only want these $100 million pictures that make $500m."

"Sometimes I feel like the movie business betrayed me, but that's kind of a whiny attitude. Basically, I don't give a fuck, because the movie business betrayed itself. It makes a lot of shit now. It's unwatchable."
Floyd Mutrux (1941), American director

"It's totally absurd for filmmakers not to be able to make films the way they want to make them. But in this business it's very common."
David Lynch (1946), American director

"I know how to deal with both nos and yesses when it comes to the thing I really understand, which is galvanizing a creative group and handling the logistic machine that effects the creative goal. But that's a lot different than dealing with Hollywood and the studio system. Each studio culture is completely different. The decisions that are made are one part business and five parts emotion, even though you're dealing with millions of dollars that can affect people's careers."
Ron Howard (1954). American actor and director

"I don't think there is an executive in this town with a decent idea, and I can't pretend that they do. I think the whole system in an insult."
Josh Becker (1958), American director

"My experience is that if your vision is strong enough – you really have a strong enough film in your head that you're trying to achieve – you'll do that no matter how many studio notes and bullshit that you get... The day I say, 'Oh the studio made me do this and this,' I'll quit."
Richard Linklater (1960), American director

"Just in general, the studio system lends itself to a lot of people who don't have that much invested in the movie but have strong opinions, and they go home at night and they don't care about the movie. And as a director, it's your life."
Frank Coraci (1966), American director

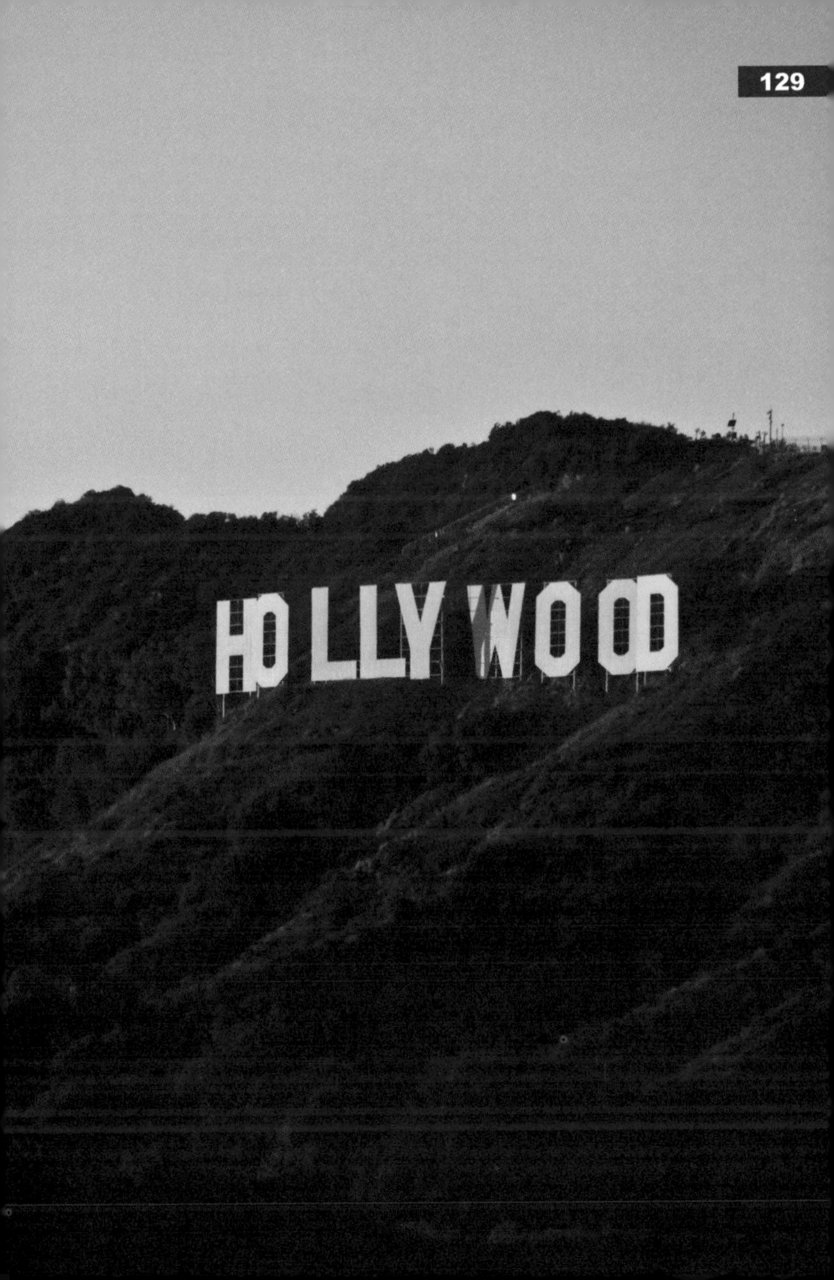
HOLLYWOOD

A GOOD SCRIPT IS HALF THE WORK

rule
44

A good script is half the work.
Or, to quote British director Ridley Scott: "The fundamental of anything as a director is material, material, material – script, script, script – once you have the script everything else is straightforward."

"With a good script, a good director can produce a masterpiece. With the same script, a mediocre director can produce a passable film. But with a bad script even a good director can't possibly make a good film. For truly cinematic expression, the camera and the microphone must be able to cross both fire and water. The script must be something that has the power to do this."

Akira Kurosawa (1910-1998),
Japanese director

"You have to have a good screenplay. This has been proven many times. No matter who you put in it, if it's got a lousy screenplay, it'll be a lousy movie! The audiences won't go."
Albert Band (1924), French-born director

"One of the advantages of the past – where the producers had the most power – was that there was generally more concern about the screenplay. Since the predominant power shifted to the directors, there has been less attention paid to the writing."
Robert Towne (1934), American screenwriter and director

"If you direct something poorly and re-shoot it the next day, stage it better, make it work better, you have a lot of possibilities. You can edit it in certain ways so that it works, but there's no getting around weaknesses of the script."
Woody Allen (1935), American director

"When you have good material, every actor wants to do it."
Tony Scott (1944), English director

"The advice I always give anybody who wants to be in film is chiefly this: script, script, script. Were it not for the script for *Clerks*, my film career would have stalled quite quickly. The fact of the matter was, we had a film with shoddy, wooden acting; flat, ugly visuals; and obvious amateurity. But critics and audiences forgave the shortcomings because they enjoyed the script. Everything else can sag a little, if the script is interesting enough."
Kevin Smith (1970), American director

Sequels Suck

rule
45

Sequels have something of a bad rep. Granted, most pale in comparison to the original, but in recent years movies like *The Dark Knight*, *Kill Bill Vol. 2* and *Toy Story 3* have disproven the myth that all sequels suck. And then there's of course the not-so-recent but no less impressive sequel *The Godfather: Part II*, which was the first sequel ever to win an Oscar for best picture.

"It's always an enormous pressure when you do a sequel. The demands are so high, and it's expensive."
Jan de Bont (1943), Dutch director

"I don't do sequels. But that's not just a blank statement. I think the reason most directors make that statement is because you've already done your hit on that idea. Is there another? I don't have another take on it. That was it. You saw it. I shot my wad."
Betty Thomas (1948), American actress and director

"By definition a sequel can't be original. So you've got to figure out what worked the first time around."
Barry Sonnenfeld (1953), American director and producer

"People are getting tired of seeing TV shows remade, or movies from the 1950s, and comic books, and sequels."
Spike Lee (1957), American director

"A FILM SHOULD STAND ON ITS OWN."

rule 46

Take David Lynch's advice to heart and ditch the director's commentary: "A film should stand on its own. It's absurd if a filmmaker needs to say what a film means in words."

"I don't do director's commentary tracks on my DVD releases... We've got to guard the film itself. It should stand alone. You work so hard to get a film a certain way; it shouldn't be fiddled with. Director's commentaries just open a door to changing people's take on the number one thing – the film. I do believe in telling stories surrounding a film, but to comment as it's rolling is a sacrilege."
David Lynch (1946), American director

"As a fan, I really appreciate all the extra material that is included on a well-thought-out DVD."
Ron Howard (1954), American actor and director

"Audiences have grown lazy because they're used to having someone else tell them what the film is supposed to represent rather than formulate their own opinions."
Frank Darabont (1959), Hungarian-American director

Never underestimate the importance of sound

Cinema a visual medium? Not according to David Lynch who once said that "Films are 50 percent visual and 50 percent sound," while adding that "sometimes sound even overplays the visual." So never underestimate the importance of film sound: from sound effects like squeaky doors, to mesmerizing voice-overs and award-winning movie scores.

———

"When the music goes on the film it's amazing how much it livens up the film and gives it an emotional kick in the pants, sort of."
Woody Allen (1935), American director

"There is the soundtrack, which might be several tracks, and the image. And without the happy marriage of those two you're not using every bit of potential that you possibly can in editing a movie."
Carol Littleton (1942), American editor

"The music has to marry with the picture and enhance it. You can't just lob something in and think it's going to work, even if it's one of your all-time-favorite songs. That piece of music may have nothing to do with the scene. When it marries, you can feel it. The thing jumps; a 'whole is greater than the sum of the parts' kind of thing can happen."
David Lynch (1946), American director

"Sound is so important to the feel of a film. To get the right presence for a room, the right feel from the outside, or the right-sounding dialogue is like playing an instrument. You have to do a lot of experimenting to get that just right."
David Lynch (1946), American director

LIGHTS, CAMERA, ACTION!

This well-known cue has been heard by crews the world over at the beginning of a new take. The phrase is believed to have been coined by American director D.W. Griffith, best known for his controversial movie *The Birth of a Nation* (1915). Griffith uttered the words on the set of *In Old California* (1910), the first movie ever made in Hollywood. The catchphrase, which caught on big time and is used to this very day, clearly demonstrates the importance of lighting in movies (or at least the importance of lighting people to take notice on set).

"I didn't know I was doing film noir, I thought they were detective stories with low lighting!"
Marie Windsor (1919-2000), American actress

"The light can make all the difference in a film, even in a character. I love seeing people come out of darkness."
David Lynch (1946), American director

"So much of movie acting is in the lighting."
Ralph Fiennes (1962), British actor

"I'm going to insult a whole industry here, but it seems like TV is for people who can't do film. I'm not talking about actresses; I'm talking about lighting people. Lighting on TV is just so... it's sinful, it really is."
Kevyn Aucoin (1962-2002), American make-up artist

Film is dead

In his book *Catching the Big Fish* director David Lynch enlightens his readers about both transcendental meditation and moviemaking, only to drop one massive bombshell at the end of his book, announcing the death of film: "I'm through with film as a medium. For me, film is dead." But fear not, Lynch is not claiming that film itself is a dying art, but rather that the days of shooting movies with 35mm film cameras, or "dinosaurs" as the acclaimed director calls them, are over.

"The cinema is an invention without a future"
Louis Lumière (1864-1948), French fimmaker

"I didn't see this the death of film coming so quickly or so sweepingly."
Roger Ebert (1942), American film critic

"Once you start working in that world of DV with small, lightweight equipment and automatic focus, working with film seems so cumbersome. These 35mm film cameras are starting to look like dinosaurs to me. They're huge; they weigh tons. And you've got to move them around. There are so many things that have to be done, and it's all so slow. It kills a lot of possibilities. With DV everything is lighter; you're more mobile. It's far more fluid."
David Lynch (1946), American director

"The birth of the talkies, it goes without saying, represents the first death of cinema... The movies survived sound, just as they survived television, the VCR and every other terminal diagnosis. And they will survive the current upheavals as well. How can I be sure? Because 10, 20, or 50 years from now someone will certainly be complaining that they don't make them like they used to. Which is to say, like they do right now."
Anthony Oliver Scott (1966), American film critic

The audience is always right

Woody Allen has gone on record stating that the audience is always right. Granted, once in a while, you get "a film that the audience is wrong about," but according to the American director "that's a rarity."

"Everybody in the audience is an idiot, but taken together they're a genius."
Billy Wilder (1906-2002), American writer and director

"An audience is never wrong. An individual member of it may be an imbecile, but a thousand imbeciles together in the dark – that is critical genius"
Billy Wilder (1906-2002), American writer and director

"The audience is not wrong."
Roger Corman (1926), American director

"A lot of films are underrated. Many just don't find their audience, and sometimes they find their audience later. Even a great film like Citizen Kane didn't find its audience until years later. It never found its full audience. It's shocking to think that it didn't open up to applause."
Harold Becker (1928), American director

"The lasting and ultimately most important reputation of a film is not based on reviews, but on what, if anything, people say about it over the years, and on how much affection for it they have."
Stanley Kubrick (1928-1999), American director

"I never read reviews. I'm not interested. But I value a lot the reactions of the spectators."
Hayao Miyazaki (1941), Japanese director

"The unfortunate thing with the studios is that they only know one audience, which is a teenage boy."
Richard Linklater (1960), American director

"If a film flops, the film was bad no matter how much you liked it. The audience is always right. Usually, actors get all the credit and the blame for a film, but it should not be like that."
Salman Khan (1965), Indian actor

Break the rules

You've got to know the rules so you can now go on and break them.

"If I'd observed all the rules, I'd never have got anywhere."
Marilyn Monroe (1926-1962), American actress

"If you want to become a filmmaker, don't let anybody tell you 'no.' Don't let anything stop you. Be persistent and do it. Set your goals and attain them."
Harold Becker (1928), American director

"People have tried to describe the film business, but it`s impossible to describe because it`s so crazy. You must know your craft inside out and then pick up the rules as you go along."
John Carpenter (1948), American director

"There are no rules. There are as many ways to make a film as there are potential filmmakers. It's an open form. Anyway, I would personally never presume to tell anyone else what to do or how to do anything. To me that's like telling someone else what their religious beliefs should be. Fuck that... If anyone tells you there is only one way, their way, get as far away from them as possible, both physically and philosophically."
Jim Jarmusch (1953), American director

"Essentially filmmaking is very simple. There are rules to be learnt, and you can learn stuff about lenses and cameras and things, but actually the basic rules are very simple. If there was ever a time when you could just pick up a camera and do it, it's now. So that's a bit of advice I can pass on – in the Nike fashion, just do it!"
Marc Evans (1963), Welsh director

CONTRIBUTORS

1 Viktor Hertz
(www.viktorhertz.com)

2 Jerod Gibson
(http://jerodgibson.com)

3 Teo Zirinis
(http://handsoffmydinosaur.tumblr.com)

4 Ged Carroll (cc)
(http://renaissancechambara.jp)

5 Derek Eads
(http://derekeads.tumblr.com)

6 Thomas Crenshaw (cc)
(www.flickr.com/photos/tommyc)

7 Joel Robison
(www.flickr.com/photos/joel_r)

8 Markee, advertising agency
(www.markee.be)

9 Wolfgang Hermann (cc)
(www.flickr.com/photos/wolfgangfoto)

10 Paul Sapiano (cc)
(http://flavors.me/peasap)

11 Yi Chen (cc)
(www.flickr.com/photos/yiie)

12 Bart-Jan Steerenberg
(www.deviator.nl)

13 Chi King (cc)
(www.flickr.com/photos/davelau)

26 MOK designz
(www.mokdesignz.nl)
27 Nicola since 1972 (cc)
(www.flickr.com/photos/15216811@N06)
28 Oscar Delmar
(http://oscardelmar.com)
29 James Bowe (cc)
(www.flickr.com/photos/jamesrbowe)
30 Mille Dørge
(www.milled.dk)
31 Suicine
http://www.flickr.com/photos/bigmikeyeah/
32 JD Hancock (cc)
(www.flickr.com/photos/jdhancock/

33 Project & concept by
Woes van Haaften / Incl. *(www.i-n-c-l.nl)*
Illustration by Ferry Bertholet
Screen printed by Kees Maas / Interbellum
34 Mike Jennings (cc)
(www.flickr.com/photos/tymcode)
35 DTM_INC
(www.behance.net/dtm_inc)
36 Alvaro Tapia Hidalgo
(www.alvarotapia.com)

INDEX BY NAME

Also available

Never Use White Type on a Black Background
And 50 other Ridiculous Design Rules

"One of the most fun and quirky books one can read about rules in the world of fashion and design. Great for a laugh and to challenge your thinking and pre-conceptions as a designer."
- Design Indaba Magazine

ISBN 978 90 6369 207 0

Never Leave the House Naked
And 50 other Ridiculous Fashion Rules

"The book is neatly designed. Small format, great graphics and plenty of illustrations commissioned to talented young graphic designers."
- We Make Money Not Art

ISBN 978 90 6369 214 8

The Medium is the Message
And 50 other Ridiculous Advertising Rules

"The book light-heartedly pokes fun at statements that, either for good or bad, have become clichéd principles of advertising."
- Dezeen

ISBN 978 90 6369 215 5

Never Use Pop Up Windows
And 50 other Ridiculous Web Rules

"A great gift for every early adaptor you know."
- Dutch Cowgirls

ISBN 978 90 6369 217 9

Never Use More Than Two Different Typefaces
And 50 other Ridiculous Typography Rules

"A handy designer's go-to for the rules of typography. Each page is beautifully set out and thoughtfully illustrated."
- Designweek

ISBN 978 90 6369 216 2

BISPUBLISHERS
www.bispublishers.nl

Thanks to:

Premsela, Dutch Platform for Design and Fashion (www.premsela.org)

Lemon scented tea (www.lemonscentedtea.com)